D0171743

CREATE A · POEM

CREATE
A · POEM

WRITING PROMPTS FOR POETS

chartwell
books

YOU'RE A POET,
AND YOU KNOW IT

Long before we had cities of stone or the technology to write, our ancestors were expressing their wants, needs, and personalities through singing and reciting poetry. Poetry was a record of history, an art form for every age, and a weapon capable of swaying any battle. It was the simplest and most revered form of communication for centuries.

Connecting you to the legacy of poetry, this journal helps you dive into writing poems no matter your level of experience. Poems can be anything born of words—descriptions of random thoughts, simple stories, or fleeting feelings.

In this journal, you will start your writing exercise by selecting a topic that triggers an idea. Then, review the word associations and think about how each relates to the topic or any connected experiences you've had in your own life. Jot down whatever comes to mind in the space provided; disjointed thoughts and phrase or internal dialogue are all encouraged, these need not be complete sentences. Now, you're ready to put it all together in a lyrical masterpiece of your own. There are no wrong answers; each poem is unique and personal to the writer.

Let your mind wander and the creativity flow!

Create a poem about:
FAMILY

_____

_____

_____

_____

_____

_____

_____

_____

_____

_____

_____

_____

_____

_____

_____

_____

_____

_____

_____

_____

_____

_____

_____

USE THESE WORDS IN YOUR POEM:

tree, roots, ancestors,

mother, father, children,

home, name, tribe, clan

Create a poem about:
LOVE

USE THESE WORDS IN YOUR POEM:

kiss, sacrifice, romance, partner,

trust, attraction, falling, communication,

envy, compromise

Create a poem about:
DREAMS

USE THESE WORDS IN YOUR POEM:

shadows, goals, memories,

nightmares, night, hopes, anxiety,

fears, terror, victory

Create a poem about:
STRUGGLE

USE THESE WORDS IN YOUR POEM:

adversity, obstacles, goal,

perseverance, chains, shackles,

growth, chance, pain, hope

Create a poem about:
SUCCESS

Create a poem about:
CHANCE

USE THESE WORDS IN YOUR POEM:

fortune, destiny, luck, risk,

loss, gamble, gain, cliff,

odds, opportunity

Create a poem about:
FAITH

USE THESE WORDS IN YOUR POEM:

question, sin,

God, belief, truth, miracle,

religion, doubt, trust, leap

Create a poem about:
STRANGER

USE THESE WORDS IN YOUR POEM:

lonely, outsider, shadow,

unknown, darkness, mystery, new,

foreign, different, unfamiliar

Create a poem about:
TREASURE

USE THESE WORDS IN YOUR POEM:

gold, hunt, danger,

map, relic, guard, legend,

hidden, buried, pirate

Create a poem about:
MYSTERY

USE THESE WORDS IN YOUR POEM:

surprise, unexpected, curiosity,

wonder, clue, suspect,

question, riddle, darkness, secret

Create a poem about:
BODY

USE THESE WORDS IN YOUR POEM:

image, attraction,

shame, diet, strength, frailty,

beauty, size, comfort, soul

Create a poem about:
NATURE

USE THESE WORDS IN YOUR POEM:

force, beauty, instinct, violence,

chaos, human, environment,

passion, seed, weather

Create a poem about:
TECHNOLOGY

USE THESE WORDS IN YOUR POEM:

change, machines, speed, distance,

screens, space, advance,

future, drain, upgrade

Create a poem about:
PAIN

USE THESE WORDS IN YOUR POEM:

ache, grief, wound, suffer, healing,

forever, deep, torment,

sorrow, soothe

Create a poem about:
HOME

USE THESE WORDS IN YOUR POEM:

family, roots, love,

ancestor, safety, memory, growth,

loss, damage, past

Create a poem about:
HISTORY

USE THESE WORDS IN YOUR POEM:

maps, folklore, time, modern,

globe, empire, mistakes,

lessons, record, memory

Create a poem about:
FUTURE

USE THESE WORDS IN YOUR POEM:

legacy, questions, uncertainty,

hope, fear, promise, possibility,

prediction, bleak, imagination

Create a poem about:
QUEST

USE THESE WORDS IN YOUR POEM:

goal, future, adventure,

possibility, road, vision, purpose,

obstacle, story, hero

Create a poem about:
SECRETS

USE THESE WORDS IN YOUR POEM:

spy, death, reveal,

guard, protect, discovery,

mystery, hidden, trust, lies

Create a poem about:
DEATH

USE THESE WORDS IN YOUR POEM:

dark, finish, grave,

passage, Heaven, Hell,

light, ending, birth, body

Create a poem about:
Freedom

USE THESE WORDS IN YOUR POEM:

opportunity, chains, rights,

oppression, safety,

protection, trap, spirit, genie, life

Create a poem about:
POWER

USE THESE WORDS IN YOUR POEM:

hight, fall, force, strength,

sacrifice, royalty, energy,

drive, control, current

Create a poem about:
TIME

USE THESE WORDS IN YOUR POEM:

past, present, future,

watch, flow, forever, cycle,

growth, decay, legacy

Create a poem about:
FRIENDSHIP

USE THESE WORDS IN YOUR POEM:

companion, bond, share,

kindred, reciprocal, confide,

trust, mutual, memories, secrets

Create a poem about:
SPACE

USE THESE WORDS IN YOUR POEM:

time, sphere, star,

air, void, infinite, empty,

open, curtain, gravity

Create a poem about:
ART

USE THESE WORDS IN YOUR POEM:

design, pattern, color, achieve,

civilization, perspective,

abstract, creation, form, revolution

Create a poem about:
PURPOSE

USE THESE WORDS IN YOUR POEM:

goal, target, aim, arrow,

mountain, destiny, lost,

function, plan, dream

Create a poem about:
LUXURY

USE THESE WORDS IN YOUR POEM:

money, fame, big,

commercial, plastic, comfort,

fortune, worth, sloth, pleasure

Create a poem about:
PARENTING

USE THESE WORDS IN YOUR POEM:

attachment, vulnerable,

responsible, model, tired, legacy, pain,

nurture, nature, separation

Create a poem about:
AGE

USE THESE WORDS IN YOUR POEM:

development, vintage, old,

past, growth, death, mortal,

conservation, time, health

Create a poem about:
SCHOOL

USE THESE WORDS IN YOUR POEM:

competition, segregate, safety, peers,

growth, intelligence, lesson,

discipline, compulsory, class

Create a poem about:
TRANSPORTATION

USE THESE WORDS IN YOUR POEM:

port, move, travel, journey,

wheels, cycles, flight,

drive, freedom, toll

Create a poem about:
MOVEMENT

USE THESE WORDS IN YOUR POEM:

motion, revolution, resistance,

forward, progress, grace,

dance, trend, change, illusion

Create a poem about:
SHOPPING

USE THESE WORDS IN YOUR POEM:

consume, luxury, bazaar, need,

desire, appearance, social, center,

commodity, money

Create a poem about:
ESCAPE

USE THESE WORDS IN YOUR POEM:

prison, refuge, freedom,

cage, shackles, hide, run,

danger, vacation, fantasy

Create a poem about:
DIRECTION

USE THESE WORDS IN YOUR POEM:

order, map, purpose,

flow, compass, play,

dart, route, bias, pole

Create a poem about:
VOICE

USE THESE WORDS IN YOUR POEM:

mermaid, narrate, opinion,

echo, silence, accent, sing,

choke, chest, express

Create a poem about:
HABIT

USE THESE WORDS IN YOUR POEM:

routine, discipline, vice, addiction,

instinct, nun, moral,

structure, rigid, home

Create a poem about:
VEIL

USE THESE WORDS IN YOUR POEM:

shadow, bride, hide, lure,

shield, sight, mystery, transparent,

ignorance, curtain

Create a poem about:
LETTER

USE THESE WORDS IN YOUR POEM:

missive, diary, pen, will,

intent, law, note, forge,

figure, envelope

Create a poem about:
REFLECTION

USE THESE WORDS IN YOUR POEM:

mirror, ponder, thought,

meditation, twin, eye, ghost,

critique, imagine, self

Create a poem about:
TOUCH

USE THESE WORDS IN YOUR POEM:

feel, glove, bare, sense,

contact, disturb, land, effect,

power, manipulate

Create a poem about:
BIRTH

USE THESE WORDS IN YOUR POEM:

give, growth, seed, spawn,

beginning, womb, gene,

fortune, destiny, conception

Create a poem about:
FORBIDDEN

USE THESE WORDS IN YOUR POEM:

fruit, taboo, danger, ban,

rule, sin, untouchable,

snake, religion, zone

Create a poem about:
TROUBLE

USE THESE WORDS IN YOUR POEM:

punish, pain, crisis,

mischief, thief, loss, law,

rebellion, youth, mistake

Create a poem about:
CONNECTION

_____
_____
_____
_____
_____
_____
_____
_____
_____
_____
_____
_____
_____
_____
_____
_____
_____
_____
_____
_____
_____
_____
_____
_____

USE THESE WORDS IN YOUR POEM:

brain, nerve, network,

transit, mafia, plumbing,

family, blood, sever, tie

Create a poem about:
CREATION

USE THESE WORDS IN YOUR POEM:

annihilation, genesis, template,

invention, divine, embryo, clone,

experiment, myth, copyright

Create a poem about:
FURNITURE

USE THESE WORDS IN YOUR POEM:

maker, item, dealer, antique,

rearrange, polish, wood,

fashion, carve, room

Create a poem about:
WITNESS

USE THESE WORDS IN YOUR POEM:

truth, see, disappear,

vow, testify, trial, accuse,

crime, reveal, alibi

Create a poem about:
Swallow

USE THESE WORDS IN YOUR POEM:

poison, flight, draught,

serpent, pride, potion, reflex,

patient, pop, grimace

Create a poem about:
COLD

USE THESE WORDS IN YOUR POEM:

sickness, blizzard, cruel,

arctic, lifeless, distant, ruthless,

sleep, remote, final

Create a poem about:
BULLY

USE THESE WORDS IN YOUR POEM:

bystander, kid, bribe, target,

school, imbalance, rage,

security, torment, tyrant

Create a poem about:
RESOLUTION

USE THESE WORDS IN YOUR POEM:

meditation, image, scan,

telescope, decision, unanimous,

affirm, withdraw, war, vote

Create a poem about:
COMEDY

USE THESE WORDS IN YOUR POEM:

sketch, showtime, direct,

laugh, satire, gag, tragic,

art, drama, stage

Create a poem about:
FILM

USE THESE WORDS IN YOUR POEM:

stage, lens, role,

thrill, trailer, star, story,

flash, shoot, climax

Create a poem about:
DISTURBANCE

USE THESE WORDS IN YOUR POEM:

insomnia, fragment, disease,

mind, madness, sense, noise,

mood, magnet, earthquake

Create a poem about:
MATURITY

USE THESE WORDS IN YOUR POEM:

life, adulthood, seed,

potential, ripe, harvest,

age, span, account, mind

Create a poem about:
RELIABILITY

USE THESE WORDS IN YOUR POEM:

quality, stability, bias, error,

prediction, test, guarantee,

safety, foundation, sense

Create a poem about:
REASON

USE THESE WORDS IN YOUR POEM:

argument, suspect, revelation,

instinct, justice, compel, logic,

error, motive, excuse

Create a poem about:
WOMEN

USE THESE WORDS IN YOUR POEM:

life, protection, attraction,

sense, nature, sister, mother,

wife, queen, anchor

Create a poem about:
MEN

USE THESE WORDS IN YOUR POEM:

power, father, husband,

brother, son, alpha, defense,

war, provision, king

Create a poem about:
MUSIC

USE THESE WORDS IN YOUR POEM:

lyric, funk, rap, melody,

harmony, chord, note,

line, lute, band

Create a poem about:
WATER

USE THESE WORDS IN YOUR POEM:

vapor, ocean, sky,

life, cycle, shallow, sprinkle,

flow, element, flood

Create a poem about:
Nostalgia

USE THESE WORDS IN YOUR POEM:

innocence, home, childhood,

memory, lost, sense, longing,

vintage, haunt, time

Create a poem about:
HERD

USE THESE WORDS IN YOUR POEM:

immunity, beast, prey,

nomad, slaughter, steer, migrate,

tame, roam, trail

Create a poem about:
PRIDE

Create a poem about:
FOOD

_____
_____
_____
_____
_____
_____
_____
_____
_____
_____
_____
_____
_____
_____
_____
_____
_____
_____
_____
_____
_____

USE THESE WORDS IN YOUR POEM:

forage, flavor, starve,

supply, ration, market, junk, genetic,

wholesome, taboo, consume

Create a poem about:
FIGHT

USE THESE WORDS IN YOUR POEM:

duel, enemy, odds,

rebel, ally, blood, win,

surrender, number, power

Create a poem about:
CHARGE

USE THESE WORDS IN YOUR POEM:

horse, bill, electric,

murder, spy, guilt, fine,

conspire, plea, explode

Create a poem about:
Cup

USE THESE WORDS IN YOUR POEM:

coffee, hand, chalice, prize,

final, qualify, sip,

together, match, goal

Create a poem about:
MESSAGE

USE THESE WORDS IN YOUR POEM:

send, encrypt, alert,

bottle, secret, spy, prophet,

phone, deliver, signal

Create a poem about:
CRAVING

USE THESE WORDS IN YOUR POEM:

appetite, symptom, drug,

sympathy, sense, desire, body,

habit, hungry, pregnancy

Create a poem about:
BLESSING

USE THESE WORDS IN YOUR POEM:

curse, giver, pray, fortune,

supernatural, happiness, worship,

ceremony, spirit, faith

Create a poem about:
BREAKTHROUGH

USE THESE WORDS IN YOUR POEM:

enemy, success, milestone,

discovery, science, barrier, performance,

exploit, penetrate, weapon

Create a poem about:
DISTANCE

USE THESE WORDS IN YOUR POEM:

space, point, measure,

difference, line, void,

travel, emotion, pace, cold

Create a poem about:
Go

USE THESE WORDS IN YOUR POEM:

errand, wilt, bathroom,

fare, nowhere, move,

beyond, stall, travel, leave

Create a poem about:
SILENCE

USE THESE WORDS IN YOUR POEM:

sound, murmur, chatter,

solitude, echo, mute, muffle,

gene, command, secret

Create a poem about:
NOISE

USE THESE WORDS IN YOUR POEM:

roar, sound, click, rumor,

commotion, complaint, music,

crash, filter, drown

Create a poem about:
Toy

USE THESE WORDS IN YOUR POEM:

playmate, factory, stuffed,

trifle, collection, model, feeling,

manipulate, game, puppet

Create a poem about:
Guess

USE THESE WORDS IN YOUR POEM:

riddle, password, clue, doubt,

evidence, suspect, possibility,

estimate, surprise, unknown

Create a poem about:
INVENTION

USE THESE WORDS IN YOUR POEM:

monopoly, royalty, discovery,

patent, future, creation, experiment,

ease, robot, magic

Create a poem about:
SANITY

USE THESE WORDS IN YOUR POEM:

madness, chaos, erosion,

question, mind, cling, fear,

balance, mask, joker

Create a poem about:
EVOLUTION

USE THESE WORDS IN YOUR POEM:

process, human, gene,

diversity, extinction, origin, order,

body, population, ape

Create a poem about:
Light

USE THESE WORDS IN YOUR POEM:

spirit, intelligence, fire,

star, sun, window, dark,

extinguish, shadow, heart

Create a poem about:
COURAGE

USE THESE WORDS IN YOUR POEM:

hero, virtue, muster,

coward, display, fail,

spirit, danger, fear, war

Create a poem about:
CHARM

magic, witch, wit, sweet,

irresistible, attraction, power,

falter, manner, spell

Create a poem about:
DESTINY

USE THESE WORDS IN YOUR POEM:

fate, manifest, birth,

epic, course, prophecy, shape,

guide, tragic, seed

Create a poem about:
UNDERGROUND

USE THESE WORDS IN YOUR POEM:

mine, treasure, coffin,

tunnel, subway, well, crypt,

chamber, magma, fugitive

Create a poem about:
BOUNDARY

USE THESE WORDS IN YOUR POEM:

edge, coastline, frontier,

territory, fault, limit,

outlaw, cross, map, citizen

Create a poem about:
COLOR

USE THESE WORDS IN YOUR POEM:

shade, vision, race, selective,

tone, insignia, rainbow,

contrast, photo, light

Create a poem about:
BLOOM

USE THESE WORDS IN YOUR POEM:

flower, complexion, spring,

beauty, fresh, love,

season, honey, pluck, ripe

Create a poem about:
Honor

USE THESE WORDS IN YOUR POEM:

war, ceremony, legacy,

dignity, state, pledge,

king, armor, value, trust

Create a poem about:
DUTY

USE THESE WORDS IN YOUR POEM:

tax, trade, obligation,

right, responsibility, standard,

sense, guard, oath, loyalty

Create a poem about:
ORDER

USE THESE WORDS IN YOUR POEM:

sequence, arrange, public,

peace, command, freedom, service,

attack, knight, spiritual

Create a poem about:
BOTTOM

USE THESE WORDS IN YOUR POEM:

hole, layer, sense,

fall, sink, cargo, low,

despair, plug, decompose

Create a poem about:
SYMBOL

USE THESE WORDS IN YOUR POEM:

tattoo, sign, code, talisman,

metaphor, constellation, mascot, meaning,

representation, importance

Create a poem about:
CHALLENGE

USE THESE WORDS IN YOUR POEM:

duel, dare, wrestle, possession,

champion, success, opposition,

monopoly, ballot, face

Create a poem about:
CHERISH

USE THESE WORDS IN YOUR POEM:

love, dear, feeling, memory,

protect, promise, treasure,

forever, hope, care

Create a poem about:
GRATITUDE

USE THESE WORDS IN YOUR POEM:

kindness, emotion, gift,

warm, virtue, embrace,

feeling, grateful, heart, deed

Create a poem about:
GREED

USE THESE WORDS IN YOUR POEM:

possession, poison, ambition,

envy, desire, self, sin,

luxury, loot, treasure

Create a poem about:
STYLE

USE THESE WORDS IN YOUR POEM:

flair, grace, fashion,

figure, display, ornament, sign,

dress, royalty, decorate

Create a poem about:
FOLK

USE THESE WORDS IN YOUR POEM:

common, culture, tradition,

history, lore, tale, influence,

ordinary, custom, spirit

Create a poem about:
STORY

Create a poem about:
HEROISM

USE THESE WORDS IN YOUR POEM:

bravery, model, villain, fable,

legend, superhuman, tragedy,

slay, sandwich, icon

Create a poem about:
TEMPTATION

USE THESE WORDS IN YOUR POEM:

devil, lure, wild,

shame, sin, resist, snake,

craving, struggle, desire

Create a poem about:
DISCIPLINE

USE THESE WORDS IN YOUR POEM:

control, force, system,

submission, authority, train, drill,

structure, skill, prison

Create a poem about:
PUNISH

USE THESE WORDS IN YOUR POEM:

crime, justice, offense,

anger, rebel, conduct, harm,

innocent, dictator, defy

Create a poem about:
IDENTITY

USE THESE WORDS IN YOUR POEM:

theft, mask, appearance,

disguise, authentic, self, meaning,

person, privacy, proof

Create a poem about:
Loss

USE THESE WORDS IN YOUR POEM:

defeat, suffer, avenge,

devastation, grieve, balance,

sympathy, death, delete, weight

Create a poem about:
CONFUSION

USE THESE WORDS IN YOUR POEM:

clarity, misunderstand, shame,

fail, paralysis, anarchy, lost,

amnesia, blend, error

Create a poem about:
CRISIS

USE THESE WORDS IN YOUR POEM:

collapse, resolve, turn,

change, hostage, bankrupt, danger,

crucial, ultimatum, nuclear

Create a poem about:
GIFT

USE THESE WORDS IN YOUR POEM:

magic, birthday, power,

wrap, ability, festive, favor,

give, accept, exchange

Create a poem about:
MAGIC

USE THESE WORDS IN YOUR POEM:

genie, fairy, wizard,

talisman, spell, power, supernatural,

illusion, mystery, bullet

Create a poem about:
ADVICE

USE THESE WORDS IN YOUR POEM:

recommend, expert, prescribe,

sage, warning, therapy, knowledge,

wisdom, confidence, owl

Create a poem about:
SURVIVAL

USE THESE WORDS IN YOUR POEM:

life, health, essential,

predator, chance, gene, persist,

strategy, emergency, nature

Create a poem about:
VICTORY

USE THESE WORDS IN YOUR POEM:

competition, achieve, match,

podium, rival, war, race,

game, final, claim

Create a poem about:
Betrayal

USE THESE WORDS IN YOUR POEM:

enemy, trust, spy,

manipulation, traitor, vengeance,

Judas, stab, alliance, loyalty

Create a poem about:
LIE

USE THESE WORDS IN YOUR POEM:

detect, sleep, place,

mask, false, truth, deception,

snake, sneak, fake

Create a poem about:
ME

USE THESE WORDS IN YOUR POEM:

self, identity, doubt, esteem,

experience, alienation, conscience,

explain, think, inside

Create a poem about:
SCANDAL

Create a poem about:
LADDER

USE THESE WORDS IN YOUR POEM:

stair, ascend, snake,

passage, top, capture, rung,

scale, damsel, goal

Create a poem about:
FIRE

USE THESE WORDS IN YOUR POEM:

heat, flame, camp,

explode, bomb, kindle, Hell,

passion, dragon, cook

Create a poem about:
ICE

(blank lined writing space)

USE THESE WORDS IN YOUR POEM:

frost, polar, avalanche,

arctic, cone, diamond, murder,

age, pale, legend

Create a poem about:
MUTATION

Create a poem about:
PANDEMIC

USE THESE WORDS IN YOUR POEM:

zombie, spread, disaster,

victim, virus, symptom, global,

wave, cancel, panic

Create a poem about:
NEWS

USE THESE WORDS IN YOUR POEM:

document, wire, anchor,

air, leak, alert, hack,

network, fake, story

Create a poem about:
EDUCATION

_____
_____
_____
_____
_____
_____
_____
_____
_____
_____
_____
_____
_____
_____
_____
_____
_____
_____
_____
_____
_____
_____
_____
_____
_____
_____

USE THESE WORDS IN YOUR POEM:

train, skill, judgement, class,

refine, bachelor, test,

institution, program, segregate

Create a poem about:
PARADISE

USE THESE WORDS IN YOUR POEM:

afterlife, Heaven, nirvana,

angel, myth, lost, island,

extinct, reward, soul

Create a poem about:
STOLEN

USE THESE WORDS IN YOUR POEM:

dreams, crook, gem,

villain, price, ransom, lurk,

thunder, land, guard

Create a poem about:
HUMAN

USE THESE WORDS IN YOUR POEM:

robot, heart, brain,

history, evolution, alien, genome,

culture, being, condition

Create a poem about:
MONSTER

USE THESE WORDS IN YOUR POEM:

terror, beast, myth,

labyrinth, creature, truck, unleashed,

closet, hunt, supernatural

Create a poem about:
HOLIDAY

USE THESE WORDS IN YOUR POEM:

tradition, festival, celebrate,

declare, meet, season, gift,

vacation, leisure, faith

Create a poem about:
HOLY

USE THESE WORDS IN YOUR POEM:

divine, religion, spirit,

bless, book, prophet,

soul, vow, sin, angel

Create a poem about:
ENTRANCE

USE THESE WORDS IN YOUR POEM:

gate, passage, exam,

admission, mesmerize, spell,

grand, vault, illusion, cave

Create a poem about:
EDGE

USE THESE WORDS IN YOUR POEM:

razor, curve, ledge,

cliff, boundary, advantage,

mountain, desire, grass, incite

Create a poem about:
WHISPER

USE THESE WORDS IN YOUR POEM:

quiet, rumor, confidence,

kiss, breath, conscience, wind,

conceal, eerie, ghost

Create a poem about:
ECLIPSE

USE THESE WORDS IN YOUR POEM:

moon, light, black,

shadow, orbit, prediction, curse,

zodiac, obscure, heavenly

Create a poem about:
HARVEST

USE THESE WORDS IN YOUR POEM:

crop, organ, ripe,

reap, hive, yield, labor,

weed, plantation, ritual

Create a poem about:
GHOST

USE THESE WORDS IN YOUR POEM:

spirit, soul, hallucination,

mist, vengeance, haunt, death,

shadow, phantom, conjure

Create a poem about:
PERFECTION

USE THESE WORDS IN YOUR POEM:

high, excellence, quality,

harmony, transcend, spiritual,

utopia, infinite, flaw, quest

Create a poem about:
NEVER

USE THESE WORDS IN YOUR POEM:

time, mend, past,

future, mistake, forfeit, dare,

alone, will, infinity

Create a poem about:
CONTROL

USE THESE WORDS IN YOUR POEM:

placebo, influence, sphere, lever,

brake, experiment, throne,

trigger, contain, command

Create a poem about:
WAR

_____

_____

_____

_____

_____

_____

_____

_____

_____

_____

_____

_____

_____

_____

_____

_____

_____

_____

_____

_____

_____

_____

_____

_____

_____

USE THESE WORDS IN YOUR POEM:

conflict, force, clash,

tug, arm, bomb, invasion,

proxy, grave, victim

Create a poem about:
PEACE

USE THESE WORDS IN YOUR POEM:

award, relation, civil,

envoy, olive, quiet, pact,

garden, offering, go

Create a poem about:
WORK

USE THESE WORDS IN YOUR POEM:

contract, machine, clog,

task, scholar, energy, goal,

tool, art, pollution

Create a poem about:
COLLECTION

USE THESE WORDS IN YOUR POEM:

archive, catalog, library,

exhibit, tale, gallery, box,

donation, unreleased, variety

Create a poem about:
EMPTY

USE THESE WORDS IN YOUR POEM:

bladder, bag, casket,

void, hole, hollow, burden,

nest, alone, calorie

Create a poem about:
MASK

USE THESE WORDS IN YOUR POEM:

protection, face, disguise,

two-faced, replica, Halloween, gas,

vigilante, ninja, shadow

Create a poem about:
NEED

USE THESE WORDS IN YOUR POEM:

caregiver, lack, requirement,

poverty, have, dire, condition,

sufficient, motive, attention

Create a poem about:
PUZZLE

USE THESE WORDS IN YOUR POEM:

riddle, clue, game,

understand, jigsaw, tangle, discover,

mystery, chess, disturb

Create a poem about:
STAR

USE THESE WORDS IN YOUR POEM:

burn, movie, sky,

fixed, body, shine, role,

symbol, destiny, rocket

Create a poem about:
SMOKE

USE THESE WORDS IN YOUR POEM:

chimney, flame, swirl,

wisp, stale, smell, vapor,

illusion, mirror, haze

Create a poem about:
RULE

Create a poem about:
CYCLE

Create a poem about:
FEAST

USE THESE WORDS IN YOUR POEM:

banquet, meal, honor,

festive, fast, sacrifice, eyes,

invitation, community, ceremony

Create a poem about:
ANIMAL

USE THESE WORDS IN YOUR POEM:

companion, experiment, herd,

zoo, graze, tame, slaughter

pyramid, beast, kingdom

Create a poem about:
PATTERN

USE THESE WORDS IN YOUR POEM:

migration, model, disorder,

behavior, repeat, spiral, weave,

random, relationship, baldness

Create a poem about:
SCHEME

Create a poem about:
BAG

USE THESE WORDS IN YOUR POEM:

grocery, pouch, empty,

canvas, hunt, kill, possession,

breathe, carry, snatch

Create a poem about:
CULTURE

USE THESE WORDS IN YOUR POEM:

art, map, bacteria,

build, assimilate, civilization, lifestyle,

stereotype, value, character

Create a poem about:
GUILT

USE THESE WORDS IN YOUR POEM:

wrong, awareness, atonement,

jury, sin, verdict, confess,

offense, trip, haunt

Create a poem about:
MONEY

USE THESE WORDS IN YOUR POEM:

luxury, value, purse,

price, greed, steal, operation,

exchange, attraction, bank

Create a poem about:
FEAR

USE THESE WORDS IN YOUR POEM:

danger, coward, alarm,

instinct, flee, monger, superstition,

hysteria, damsel, trauma

Create a poem about:
DETAILS

USE THESE WORDS IN YOUR POEM:

small, diary, biography,

outline, whole, fact, specific,

mundane, travel, personal

Create a poem about:
JOY

USE THESE WORDS IN YOUR POEM:

feeling, tiding, fleeting,

wish, dance, buzz,

house, light, giver, cheer

Create a poem about:
STILL

USE THESE WORDS IN YOUR POEM:

calm, ache, murmur,

water, silence, time, always,

tea, picture, unchanged

Create a poem about:
BORROW

USE THESE WORDS IN YOUR POEM:

gypsy, return, seek,

debt, adopt, grammar,

deviate, beg, idea, line

Create a poem about:
SHAPE

USE THESE WORDS IN YOUR POEM:

mold, status, condition,

hammer, deform, figure, outline,

loom, influence, body

Create a poem about:
SORROW

USE THESE WORDS IN YOUR POEM:

woe, grief, pathos, strike,

deep, memory, perpetual,

dwell, tragedy, oblivion

Create a poem about:
VINTAGE

USE THESE WORDS IN YOUR POEM:

classic, history, year,

origin, noir, ripe, imprint,

reminisce, timeless, quality

Create a poem about:
MAP

USE THESE WORDS IN YOUR POEM:

visual, area, imaginary,

grid, explorer, globe, face,

territory, treasure, guide

Create a poem about:
FANTASY

USE THESE WORDS IN YOUR POEM:

dragon, nonfiction, imagination,

superhero, tale, sport, artificial,

delusion, folklore, real

Create a poem about:
FACE

USE THESE WORDS IN YOUR POEM:

beard, mask, expression,

head, image, reputation, surface,

makeup, confront, mirror

Create a poem about:
ROUTINE

_____
_____
_____
_____
_____
_____
_____
_____
_____
_____
_____
_____
_____
_____
_____
_____
_____
_____
_____
_____
_____

USE THESE WORDS IN YOUR POEM:

course, performance, drill,

dance, tedious, predictable, ordinary,

habit, sketch, check

Create a poem about:
INDISTINCT

USE THESE WORDS IN YOUR POEM:

clarity, understood, sharp,

dot, pale, haze, ghost,

memory, horizon, sound

Create a poem about:
GENE

USE THESE WORDS IN YOUR POEM:

mutant, value, therapy,

germ, human, clone, code,

blueprint, trait, repression

Create a poem about:
BOOK

USE THESE WORDS IN YOUR POEM:

word, pen, thought,

bound, burn, record, script,

travel, bet, reserve

Create a poem about:
ASH

USE THESE WORDS IN YOUR POEM:

dust, scatter, volcano,

char, revenge, element, remains,

roast, burial, footprint

Create a poem about:
WILL

USE THESE WORDS IN YOUR POEM:

puppet, intention, decision,

divine, death, inheritance, destiny,

wish, part, power

Create a poem about:
ISLAND

USE THESE WORDS IN YOUR POEM:

ocean, stranded, surround,

isolation, chain, exotic, sun,

species, quarantine, resort

Create a poem about:
CENTER

USE THESE WORDS IN YOUR POEM:

detention, middle, between,

training, correction, ball,

pitch, moderate, attention

Create a poem about:
GAME

Create a poem about:
BALANCE

USE THESE WORDS IN YOUR POEM:

scale, gravity, harmony,

opposition, equal, budget, diet,

chemistry, neutral, cosmos

Create a poem about:
ENTERTAINMENT

USE THESE WORDS IN YOUR POEM:

amusement, pleasure, spectator,

casino, film, brand, perform,

diversion, talent, business

Create a poem about:
ROOM

USE THESE WORDS IN YOUR POEM:

space, distance, roof, frame,

forum, tenant, separation,

service, mate, lock

Create a poem about:
PLANT

USE THESE WORDS IN YOUR POEM:

seed, bulb, vine, herb,

forest, branch, nursery,

fungus, spy, foot

Create a poem about:
LINES

USE THESE WORDS IN YOUR POEM:

mark, continue, dimension,

commute, figure, geography, rope,

communication, border, ancestor

Create a poem about:
CHORE

USE THESE WORDS IN YOUR POEM:

errand, sing, novice, fix,

childhood, task, routine,

Cinderella, neglect, robot

Create a poem about:
NEW

USE THESE WORDS IN YOUR POEM:

creation, discovery, strange,

origin, condition, improve, time,

update, radical, seed

Create a poem about:
DESIRE

USE THESE WORDS IN YOUR POEM:

snare, motive, vice,

resist, romance, devil, craving,

siren, indulge, temptation

Create a poem about:
PIECE

(blank lined page)

USE THESE WORDS IN YOUR POEM:

quilt, scroll, puzzle, coin,

gun, pawn, patch,

together, discover, arrange

Create a poem about:
MATCH

USE THESE WORDS IN YOUR POEM:

spark, feud, marriage,

equal, contest, pair, ignite,

score, tie, replica

Create a poem about:
ENOUGH

USE THESE WORDS IN YOUR POEM:

adequate, amount, snap,

purpose, load, burden, threshold,

meter, edge, full

Create a poem about:
TRAP

USE THESE WORDS IN YOUR POEM:

snare, lure, hole, trick,

hunt, escape, wolf,

avalanche, spring, release

Create a poem about:
BEAUTY

USE THESE WORDS IN YOUR POEM:

dazzle, perception, enchantment,

beast, pageant, flower, mark,

standard, makeup, plastic

Create a poem about:
INTENTION

USE THESE WORDS IN YOUR POEM:

goal, mind, focus, suspicion,

murder, motive, evidence,

display, moral, pledge

Create a poem about:
HELP

USE THESE WORDS IN YOUR POEM:

savior, aid, disaster,

build, cry, offer, lobby,

self, negotiate, mend

Create a poem about:
LIFE

USE THESE WORDS IN YOUR POEM:

state, spirit, body,

destiny, memory, time, sacrifice,

purpose, existence, death

Inspiring | Educating | Creating | Entertaining

Brimming with creative inspiration, how-to projects, and useful
information to enrich your everyday life, Quarto Knows is a favorite
destination for those pursuing their interests and passions. Visit our
site and dig deeper with our books into your area of interest:
Quarto Creates, Quarto Cooks, Quarto Homes, Quarto Lives,
Quarto Drives, Quarto Explores, Quarto Gifts, or Quarto Kids.

© 2021 by Quarto Publishing Group USA Inc.

First published in 2021 by Chartwell Books, an imprint of The Quarto Group,
142 West 36th Street, 4th Floor, New York, NY 10018, USA
T (212) 779-4972 F (212) 779-6058 www.QuartoKnows.com

All rights reserved. No part of this journal may be reproduced in any form without written permission of the copyright
owners. All images in this journal have been reproduced with the knowledge and prior consent of the artists concerned,
and no responsibility is accepted by producer, publisher, or printer for any infringement of copyright or otherwise,
arising from the contents of this publication. Every effort has been made to ensure that credits accurately comply with
information supplied. We apologize for any inaccuracies that may have occurred and will resolve inaccurate or missing
information in a subsequent reprinting of the journal.

Chartwell titles are also available at discount for retail, wholesale, promotional, and bulk purchase. For details, contact
the Special Sales Manager by email at specialsales@quarto.com or by mail at The Quarto Group, Attn: Special Sales
Manager, 100 Cummings Center Suite 265D, Beverly, MA 01915 USA.

10 9 8 7 6 5 4 3 2 1

ISBN: 978-0-7858-3916-3

Publisher: Rage Kindelsperger
Creative Director: Laura Drew
Managing Editor: Cara Donaldson
Text: Sarosh Arif
Cover and Interior Design: B. Middleworth

Printed in China